Mysterious Encounters

LEPRECHAUNS

by Lori Mortensen

KIDHAVEN PRESS
A part of Gale, Cengage Learning

GALE
CENGAGE Learning

Detroit • New York • San Francisco • New Haven, Conn • Waterville, Maine • London

GALE
CENGAGE Learning·

Picture Credits:
Cover: ©Swim Ink 2, LLC/Corbis; AP Images, 23; © Bettmann/Corbis, 8, 37; Jim Commentucci/Syracuse Newspapers/The Image Works, 39; Mansell/Time Life Pictures/Getty Images, 16; Mary Evans Picture Library, 10; Mary Evans Picture Library/The Image Works, 12, 33, 34; Paul McErlane/Getty Images, 24; © Robert Harding World Imagery/Corbis, 17; Ronald Martinez/Getty Images, 5; © Royalty-Free/Corbis, 19, 28; Tim Boyle/Newsmakers/Getty Images, 7; Topham/The Image Works, 26

LIBRARY OF CONGRESS CATALOGING-IN-PUBLICATION DATA

Mortensen, Lori, 1955-
  Leprechauns / by Lori Mortensen.
    p. cm. — (Mysterious encounters)
  Includes bibliographical references and index.
    ISBN 13: 978-0-7377-3663-2 (hardcover)
  1. Leprechauns—Juvenile literature. 2. Fairies—Ireland—Juvenile literature. 3. Tales—Ireland. 4. Ireland—Folklore. I. Title.
  GR153.5.M67 2007
  398.21—dc22
                                                                          2007006889

ISBN-10: 0-7377-3663-1

Printed in the United States of America
2 3 4 5 6 7 12 11 10 09 08

Contents

Chapter 1

Legendary Little People

When people think of leprechauns they imagine happy little fellows dressed in green. It is not surprising. One of the most popular images of a leprechaun was created in 1964 when General Mills introduced L.C. Leprechaun (later called Lucky) on boxes of Lucky Charms cereal. More people met this famous leprechaun in television commercials that showed children chasing Lucky as he cried, "They're after me Lucky Charms!"

General Mills did not invent leprechauns, however. This character was based on tales and legends that have been told for thousands of years.

What Is a Leprechaun?

According to legend, a leprechaun is an Irish fairy. Details about leprechauns vary. Many legends describe leprechauns as **solitary** fairies that live underground in mounds, caves, holes and **bogs**. Yet other stories say

A modern-day leprechaun image: that of the University of Notre Dame mascot.

leprechauns live in groups and may dwell above ground in abandoned churches, castles, and even old kettles.

Legends also differ about leprechaun **gender**. Some legends claim there are only male leprechauns. Others say there are male *and* female leprechauns.

And while legends agree leprechauns are small, no one agrees on how small. In some tales leprechauns are no bigger than a thumbnail. In other tales leprechauns are as tall as a young child.

Descriptions about how leprechauns look and dress differ, too. In some tales leprechauns are blonde and fair. In other legends they look like little old men with beards. Their wrinkled skin may be brown or gray and their noses are red or pointy. Male leprechauns often wear tall hats, belted jackets, pants, long woolen stockings, and shoes. Yet, in other accounts they wear pants and boots without any shirt at all. Female leprechauns wear dresses. Leprechauns wear all green or combinations of red, green, brown, black, and blue.

Details about leprechaun habits vary as well. In some stories leprechauns are neat and clean. Yet, in other tales they are **foulmouthed**, and their clothes are dirty and worn. Twigs and leaves stick in their hair and they never bathe because they are afraid of water.

Leprechauns are often associated with the Irish holiday of St. Patrick's Day.

Erin go Bragh

Hurrah for mother Erin, St Patrick's Day
For her sons and daughters scattered far away
For her harp and her emblem—the shamrock green
and for the best of all—her Irish Colleen.

There is also disagreement about how leprechauns spend their time. According to some tales, leprechauns are busy shoemakers who guard pots of gold buried all over Ireland. If a **mortal** catches a leprechaun, the leprechaun must reveal the location of the treasure.

Descriptions of leprechauns differ, but commonly male leprechauns are described as wearing tall hats, belted jackets, pants, long woolen stockings, and shoes.

Although there are many tales about people catching leprechauns, hardly any tales report people getting the treasure. That is because leprechauns are too clever to lose their gold to mortals. According to legend, all a leprechaun has to do is make a mortal look away. Then in a flash, the leprechaun disappears. Other legends say leprechauns keep their pot of gold at the end of the rainbow. But no matter how long mortals chase it, they never reach it and must give up, leaving empty-handed.

Other tales say leprechauns are so rich they do not have to work at all. They while away their time smoking clay pipes, drinking **poteen**, singing, dancing, and stirring up trouble by jumping on sheep, goats, dogs, and fowl and taking them on wild rides through the fields. Other times they make mischief indoors by making babies fall, pots boil over, milk sour, and things mysteriously disappear.

History of Leprechauns

Nobody knows exactly when stories about leprechauns began. Long ago, leprechauns went by different names in different areas of Ireland. Cluricaunes, luricanes, lurikeens, and lubberkins are just a few of the names they were called. They were not called leprechauns until the late seventeenth and early eighteenth centuries. Historians believe this word came from the Irish words *leath bhrogan* (la-VRO-gahn) for "shoemaker" or *lu-acharma'n* (LOOH-ar-mahn) for "small body." Some ancient texts suggest there may have been a real race of

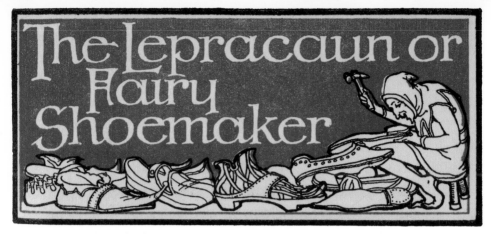

The Lepracaun or Fairy Shoemaker

Historians believe the word *leprechaun* comes from the Irish words *leath bhrogan* for "shoemaker" or *luacharma'n* for "small body."

small people who lived long ago. Legends say these little people had magical powers and could grant skills such as swimming or walking on water.

Others suggest leprechauns may have come from an ancient race of gods called Tuatha de Danann (TOO-a-ha day DONN-ann). When Christians came to Ireland in the fifth century, they told the people to stop believing in spirits and false gods. As people stopped worshipping the gods, the gods grew smaller and smaller and became fairies.

Some people claim leprechauns are fallen angels. Long ago during the war in heaven, angels had to decide whether they would follow **Lucifer** to hell or stay with God in heaven. The ones who could not decide became fallen angels. "They were angels, sure enough," said an old woman in North Antrim (Ireland), "but they would not stand with God against the Devil, and so they were put into the world of men. They became fairies over time."[1]

Still others believe leprechauns are spirits of the dead. If they were like ghosts, it would explain why they could appear and disappear in the blink of an eye.

Are Leprechauns Real?

Today, few people believe leprechauns are real, and most think they never existed. When someone claims to have seen one, people may take it as a joke, or they may say the person was probably just imagining it. Yet only 100 years ago many people believed leprechauns were real. They believed an encounter with a leprechaun could make them rich—or miserable if the leprechaun was angry.

During the eighteenth and nineteenth centuries, writers began to collect stories from people who said they had seen leprechauns. One of the earliest writers was an Oxford scholar named W.Y. Evans-Wentz. He spent several months walking from cottage to cottage talking to people throughout the British Isles. When he finished, he published a book in 1911 called *Fairy Faith in Celtic Countries.* The stories Evans-Wentz collected showed people's belief in leprechauns and other fairies and how this belief influenced everyday life. "As children we were always afraid of fairies," said one, "and were taught to say, 'God bless *them!* God bless *them!*' whenever we heard them mentioned."[2]

"If anything like dirty water was thrown out of doors after dark," said another, "it was necessary to say 'Hugga, hugga salach!' as a warning to the fairies not to get their clothes wet."[3]

"Untasted food, like milk," another related, "used to be left on the table at night for the fairies. If you were eating and food fell from you, it was not right to take it back, for the fairies wanted it."[4]

So many people told Evans-Wentz stories about fairies he was convinced invisible beings such as leprechauns and other fairies really did exist. He be-

An Irish luricane rides on a dog.

lieved they lived in the **Otherworld**, a world that overlapped this one.

Nearly a century later some people still believe in leprechauns. One expert explained that the belief in fairies never died because people kept seeing them. Not everyone who believes in leprechauns is willing to admit it, however. In the 1940s an Irish writer once asked a woman who lived in Cork if she believed in fairies. "I do not," she replied after pondering the question, "but they're there."[5]

Chapter 2

Leprechaun Sightings

Leprechaun sightings have been reported for thousands of years. Many of them occur in Ireland, but they are also reported in other countries as well. Details about sightings vary. For instance, some legends say leprechauns are only seen at night after it rains. Yet other legends say leprechauns appear during the day, too. In fact, some sightings are not sightings at all. Instead of seeing leprechauns, people have reported hearing their voices or the sounds of leprechauns singing and playing music on fiddles, pipes, and harps.

Lewis Chessmen Leprechauns

One unusual leprechaun encounter occurred in 1831 on the Isle of Lewis in the northern part of Scotland. According to legend, a worker was walking along the shore when he spied the opening to a small cave that had been exposed by a recent storm. Curious, he peered inside. To his surprise he saw a "large beehive-shaped dwelling made out of clay deep in the interior of the cave."[6] Thinking treasure might be inside, the worker grabbed a tool and smashed the object open. At once, cries filled the air like the drone of a thousand bees. Terrified, the man raced home. Even though he did not see them, he was sure he had angered leprechauns.

Out of This World

Chemicals called hallucinogens can cause people to see things that are not there. Some people have reported seeing little people after taking drugs containing hallucinogens and do not believe they were hallucinating, or seeing things that are not really there. They believe the drug opened their minds, allowing them to see things that cannot be seen in the normal world.

The Lewis Chessmen, ivory chess pieces found on the Isle of Lewis that many people believe were carved by leprechauns.

His wife was disappointed because he did not find the leprechauns' treasure and insisted he go back. When he returned he saw what appeared to be dozens of leprechauns in the cave. Upon closer inspection he discovered the leprechauns were really figures carved out of walrus ivory. There were 93 of them.

Today, these figures are on display at the British Museum as the Lewis Chessmen. Experts date the figures to the eleventh or twelfth century. Nobody knows who made them. But some people on the Isle of Lewis believe a leprechaun who lived in the windswept dunes long ago made the enchanting figures.

Not a Plastic Garden Gnome

Mary Treadgold reported an equally strange modern sighting on April 30, 1973, near the town of Mull in the Scottish Highlands. Mary was riding a bus when she glanced out the window and saw a

> small figure, about 18 inches high, a young man with his foot on a spade, arrested in the act of digging. He had a thin, keen face, tight, brown, curly hair, was dressed in bright blue **bib-and-braces**, with a very white shirt with rolled-up sleeves. An open sack, also miniature, stood at his side. He was emphatically not a dwarf, nor a child, nor a plastic garden gnome. He was a perfectly formed living being like any of us, only in miniature.[7]

A castle in the Scottish Highlands near the town of Mull, where Mary Treadgold reported seeing a leprechaun in 1973.

When Mary arrived home she contacted a friend from the Highlands and told her what she had seen. Her friend told her others had seen these little people in Mull and the town was known for such sightings.

The Vanishing Pipe

Fifteen-year-old Brian Collins reported a sighting in the early 1990s when he was on a trip with his parents in the Aran Islands on the west coast of Ireland. While he was walking he saw two leprechauns about as tall as children, fishing on an overlooking bank. They were dressed in green and wore brown boots. Brian heard them speaking, but he did not understand them because they were speaking **Gaelic**.

As soon as they spotted Brian they jumped off the bank and vanished. Brian went to the riverbank to try to find them, but all he found was a pipe. He locked the pipe in a drawer, but when he looked for it later, it was gone. Brian claimed he saw them again and took their picture and recorded their voices. But neither the pictures nor the recording showed any evidence they had been there at all.

March of the Leprechauns

An American sighting occurred in 1919 when thirteen-year-old Harry Anderson walked down a country road one summer night near Barron, Wisconsin. To his surprise he saw twenty little men

A "Leprechaun crossing" sign hopes to attract curious tourists to a town in Ireland.

marching toward him in the moonlight. All the little men were bald, and the only clothes they wore were leather pants held up by suspenders. As they walked past him Harry heard them mumbling, but they did not seem to be talking to each other. Nor were they talking to him. In fact, they walked by as if they did not see him at all. The sight of the little men was so unsettling, Harry kept walking and never looked back.

Rough River Leprechauns

Stephen Wagner reported a mysterious sighting on June 24, 2003, while he was canoeing on the Rough River in western Kentucky. He was not too far from the Rough River State Park when he had a "very funny, queasy, nervous feeling. I was inexplicably [unexplainably] anxious for some reason. Although I could not define why, I felt like I had something to fear and I sensed death."[8]

Putting his fears aside, Stephen paddled for a few more miles, then tied his canoe to a tree and went for a hike. While he was walking he spotted a clay jar in the creek. Curious, he climbed down the muddy bank to investigate. To his surprise he discovered the jar was covered with little handprints. At first he thought raccoons made the prints, but when he looked closer he realized they were tiny human handprints.

"When I at last managed to pull the crock jar out of the mud, something screamed! It sounded like a little girl, really high-pitched and loud!"[9] Stephen grabbed the jar and scrambled back up the bank.

After a few moments he set the jar down and walked along the creek to see if anyone was there.

"When I looked over that bank," Stephen reported, "I saw two little people standing about 10 inches tall. . . . They had pale skin, little brown leather pants held up by suspenders, no shirts and little pointy hats made of what looked like leather. They had leather foot coverings that went up past the ankle. Their hair was a reddish color and their eyes blue. Their hands were only about an inch wide."[10]

The little men laughed as they pulled a stump up the bank. But when Stephen glanced back to where he had left the jar, he saw three more little men. They had pushed the jar back into the creek. "Then I heard a loud snap . . . and they were all gone."[11]

Stephen later hiked back to the muddy creek to try to find the little men again, but like so many other sightings, the leprechauns and the jar had vanished.

Chapter 3

Tricks and Treasure

L egends tell of people not only seeing leprechauns but catching them as well. According
to legend, if a mortal captures a leprechaun,
the little person must give his treasure to whomever
caught him. To keep the leprechaun from escaping,
mortals need only keep their eyes on the little man.
But just when people think they will get rich, the
leprechaun tricks them and escapes.

The Leprechaun of Carberry Castle

In a tale told in Kildare, Ireland, a young girl named
Bridget went walking one summer morning in 1866

Students celebrate St. Patrick's Day by searching for four-leaf clovers, a symbol of good luck.

to fill her pitcher at the well. On her way she spied a little old leprechaun boring holes in a shoe under a thornbush. With a jug of poteen resting by his side, he sang and smoked his pipe while he worked. Seeing her chance to get rich, Bridget grabbed him by the neck and demanded his treasure.

At first the leprechaun scolded her for treating him so roughly and invited her to sit down for a chat. When she refused, he claimed he was simply a poor shoemaker. Shoemakers like himself did not

A leprechaun figure adorns this pot of shamrocks, the symbol of Ireland.

have treasure. If she let him go, he would turn his pockets out and show her.

Bridget knew he was trying to trick her. "That won't do," she said. "My eyes'll keep going through you like darning needles till I have the gold." [12]

Finally, the leprechaun admitted there might be treasure under Carberry Castle on the other side of the hill. He told her that they would have to walk there and that he would gladly show her the way if she put him down. Determined to watch for the leprechaun's tricks, Bridget gripped the leprechaun tighter and said she would carry him.

Just as they reached the top of the hill, the leprechaun cried, "Oh, murder! Castle Carberry is afire." [13] In an instant, Bridget's eyes darted toward the castle, and the leprechaun vanished.

Sean and the Bush

A legend with painful consequences is told about a young man named Sean. He was resting in a field listening to birds sing when he heard a tap, tap, tapping sound in a nearby bush. Curious, he got up and peered inside. To his amazement he saw a leprechaun sitting on a mushroom while hammering on a shoe. Below him lay pairs of boots and other fairy shoes.

Quick as a wink, Sean grabbed the leprechaun and demanded his gold. The leprechaun became angry and swore he was only a shoemaker with tools and leather. He said he did not have any gold.

Sean said he could not be fooled and insisted the leprechaun give him his treasure.

Apparently outsmarted, the leprechaun agreed and told Sean the gold was buried beneath a bush by the river. After a long walk, they arrived at the river. Sean reached into the bush—and screamed!

A tiny leprechaun crafts a pair of shoes.

Instead of finding gold, he had thrust his hand into a hive of bees. The moment Sean looked away, the leprechaun disappeared.

The Red Ribbon Leprechaun

Another leprechaun legend is so popular, it is told throughout Ireland. Details vary depending on where it is told, but each version shows how difficult it is for mortals to outwit a clever leprechaun.

According to the tale told in Kerry, Ireland, there once was a man who lived with his old mother and blind sister. The man and his family were poor as church mice, and their clothes were tattered and torn.

One day the man went out to the bog to cut peat for fuel. While he was cutting, he saw something move under the brush. Much to his surprise a leprechaun no bigger than his finger sprang out. The leprechaun wore a wide-brimmed hat and a swallow-tailed coat.

The man knew his family's problems would be over if he caught the leprechaun. So, quick as a flash he grabbed the little man by his coattails and held him fast. The leprechaun moaned and groaned about his misfortune. What a shame it was, he cried, that innocent travelers could not go about their business without being set upon by bandits.

The man shook his head. He said if anyone was innocent, it certainly was not the leprechaun, and he should show him his gold at once.

The leprechaun insisted he was only a tradesman and did not have a pot of gold. He said if the man was any sort of a gentleman at all, he would put him down and let him be on his way.

But the more the leprechaun argued, the angrier the man became. Finally, the man tightened his fist and demanded the leprechaun show him his gold immediately. Choking and sputtering, the leprechaun agreed he might have a bit of gold after all. It was not here, of course. But he would gladly show the way.

The man made sure he kept his eyes on the leprechaun as they marched down the road. Finally, the leprechaun pointed to a tree in a forest and said the treasure was buried beneath the roots. Certain the leprechaun would try to trick him, the man demanded to see the treasure. After all, the leprechaun could say it was under any tree, and how would the man know?

According to some tales, leprechauns guard pots of gold buried all over Ireland.

Leprechaunism

Were people with leprechaunism once mistaken for leprechauns? Also known as Donohue syndrome, people with this rare disease are small and have elfin features such as flared nostrils and thick lips.

With a wave of the leprechaun's hand, the man saw pots of gold lying beneath the roots of the tree. Gold coins spilled from every pot. The man gasped at the fortune. It was more treasure than he had ever imagined. Still, he refused to release the leprechaun. After all, as soon as the man left to get a shovel, he reasoned, the leprechaun would move the treasure somewhere else.

The leprechaun promised he would not lay a finger on the treasure and demanded to be let go. The man could not help but worry. Even if the leprechaun promised not to move the treasure, all the trees looked alike. Then he had an idea.

The man tore a strip of red cloth from his shirt and tied it to the tree. As an added precaution, the man made the leprechaun swear another promise. The leprechaun agreed and swore by St. Patrick and all the holy saints he would not lay a finger on the treasure or the cloth. Satisfied at last, the man released the leprechaun and raced home for a shovel.

When he returned, however, the man was shocked. The leprechaun had indeed kept his promise—he had not laid a finger on the cloth. Instead, he had tied an identical strip of cloth around every tree. The man dug about, but it was no use. The treasure was lost. Like so many others before, the leprechaun had tricked the man out of his treasure.

Chapter 4

Curse of the Leprechaun

Encounters with leprechauns are not always about mortals demanding treasure. Legends reveal leprechauns and humans may also have pleasant exchanges. For example, after a leprechaun drinks a bit, he may offer someone a drink along with some magic coins. One legend tells of a poor **nobleman** who gave a wee man a ride on his horse. The next morning the nobleman found his drafty castle filled to the rafters with gold.

Leprechaun in a Cage

Yet, for most mortals an encounter with a leprechaun has severe consequences. In 1907 a writer named Lady Archibald Campbell interviewed a poor blind man and his wife who lived in an Irish glen. The man revealed the misfortune that occurred when they captured a leprechaun.

"I gripped him close in my arms and took him home," the old man related.

> I called to the woman [his wife] to look at what I had got. "What doll is it that you have there?" she cried. "A living one," I said, and put it on the dresser. We feared to lose it; we kept the door locked. It talked and muttered to itself queer words. . . . It might have been near on a fortnight [two weeks] since we had the fairy, when I said to the woman, "Sure, if we show it in the great city we will be made up [rich]." So we put it in a cage. At night we would leave the cage door open, and we would hear it stirring through the house. . . . We fed it on bread and rice and milk out of a cup at the end of a spoon.[14]

After the leprechaun escaped, the man lost his sight and the couple's money dwindled away until they were left in poverty.

Billy Mac Daniel and the Leprechaun

Billy Mac Daniel of Cork was another mortal who supposedly suffered because of a leprechaun. Ac-

Not all leprechaun encounters have bad consequences. Here, Lusmore the Hunchback agrees to build some leprechauns a dancing floor; in return they agree to make him handsome.

cording to legend, it all began one night as Billy walked home. He had been drinking with friends and had not spent a penny. Still, it was chilly and he wished he had one more drink to warm his bones.

He no sooner wished, than he met a leprechaun with a glass of whiskey in his hand. Even though

Billy knew better than to meddle with leprechauns, when the leprechaun offered him the glass, Billy drained it in one gulp.

Unlike Billy's friends, the leprechaun demanded payment. "Out with your purse," said the leprechaun, "and pay me like a gentleman." [15] Billy replied the leprechaun should be giving him money, not the other way around.

An Irishman is surprised to find himself surrounded by leprechauns.

Angered, the leprechaun cursed Billy and declared he would be the leprechaun's servant for seven years and a day. Night after night, the little man forced Billy to gather **rushes** from a bog. The leprechaun turned the plants into magic horses. Then Billy and the leprechaun rode from house to house and drank wine cellars dry.

One night the leprechaun said it would soon be his 1,000th birthday, and he wanted to take a bride. Billy followed the leprechaun to a fine home where a bride was enjoying her bridal feast. The leprechaun knew that if she sneezed three times without a blessing, she would be his.

The girl sneezed once, then twice, without a blessing. But on the third sneeze Billy felt so sorry for a bride marrying a 1,000-year-old leprechaun, he burst out, "God save us all!" The leprechaun was so enraged he walloped Billy with his boot and fired him from his service.

Dance, Dance, Dance

One of the most tragic tales of a leprechaun encounter comes from the Bog of Allen in Ireland. According to this tale, a young girl named Kate went to a fair with her sweetheart. On the way home they got into an argument. She was so angry she jumped down from the horse-drawn cart and stormed down the road. He agreed a long walk would cool her temper and drove home without her.

Had she not been so hasty, she might have thought twice about jumping off into the bog. But her temper ruled her head, and now she had no choice but to walk home. So Kate walked down the lonely road.

To her dismay, she was still far from home when night fell and a storm brewed. Anxious to get out of the wind and rain, she looked for shelter and saw a light in a window far out in the bog. Getting there was difficult since the path was choked with reeds.

Finally, she came to a little house made of **sod** deep in the heart of the bog. There in the front door, smoking his pipe, sat a little man with a beard. Light from his flickering fire revealed his eyes, as black as ink, and his tanned skin. At his feet lay an old fiddle and bow.

Kate explained her situation and asked if she could share his floor and the warmth of the fire until morning. The little man told her he would gladly share what he had, but on a night such as this there would be little sleeping. His neighbors would soon be gathering for a night of merriment. She was welcome to join them if she liked.

Kate happily agreed and was soon dancing to the little man's lively fiddle tunes along with the other neighbors that lived in the bog. Strangely, she realized she was the only girl among them. All of the neighbors were little old men, only as big as a child.

But with all the merry music, it hardly seemed to matter. It simply gave her more reason to dance, for as soon as one small partner left, another took his place. If she stopped to catch her breath, her companions offered her cups of poteen until she was back on her feet. And so it went until the girl was so exhausted she collapsed at the door of the little sod house.

When Kate awoke she was alone in the middle of the bog. There was no sod house or neighbor to be seen. And her feet! She had danced so much her feet were raw and bloody, and her toes were nearly worn away. It was then, of course, Kate realized she had been in the company of leprechauns.

A sod house in an Irish bog, similar to the house in the story of Kate Cosendine.

With no other course, she limped back to the road and started home. Yet even this was no comfort, for as she made her way, nothing seemed familiar. Houses dotted once empty fields, and strangers passed without a glance.

Finally, however, she came to her own gate and hobbled to the door. But to her surprise a strange woman met her at the door. Kate claimed it was her house, and the woman disagreed. After all, she had lived there for the past twenty years, she said.

At last, Kate told the woman her name. The woman gasped, for her grandmother had often told her about Kate Cosendine, the girl who had disappeared from the fair so long ago.

Things were far worse than Kate imagined. When the woman showed her a mirror, Kate saw she was no longer a young girl. Staring back from the mirror was an old hag with sagging skin and tangled gray hair.

With no other choice, Kate wandered wearily through the streets. As the sun sank, she came upon a church. As she staggered up the steps, she heard the priest call a blessing on the congregation. Kate Cosendine fell to dust, at rest at last.

Leprechaun Watch

To this day, people still debate whether leprechauns exist or not. Many people have claimed to see them. Many others think people may have seen something, but it was not a leprechaun. "People see, or think

Many Irish pubs, such as Coleman's Pub in Syracuse, New York, have leprechaun doors. These tiny doors let leprechauns know they are welcome in that pub.

they see, all kinds of strange things," writes author Jerome Clark, "and among the strange things people think they see are fairies."[16]

In 2005 people in Ireland set up Leprechaun Watches to record leprechauns. They hid a series of video cameras where people believed leprechauns lived. A young landowner requested one camera. He had destroyed a stone wall and cut down a tree many believed belonged to the little people. Soon after, the family's herd of cattle died, and they suffered many misfortunes. Their neighbors are sure this was the leprechauns' way of striking back for the damage he had caused.

In spite of all the legends told about leprechauns, nobody can say for sure whether they exist or not. Some people claim they exist, and others say they do not. But whether the stories are true or not, there is no doubt that as long as there are leprechaun sightings, some people will continue to believe in the magical little people known as leprechauns.

Notes

Chapter 1: Legendary Little People

1. Quoted in Bob Curran, *The Truth About the Leprechaun*. Dublin, Ireland: Wolfhound, 2000, p. 9.
2. Quoted in W.Y. Evans-Wentz, *Fairy Faith in Celtic Countries*. New York: University Books, 1966, p. 70.
3. Evans-Wentz, *Fairy Faith in Celtic Countries*, p. 70.
4. Evans-Wentz, *Fairy Faith in Celtic Countries*, p. 70.
5. Quoted in Steenie Harvey, "Twilight Places," *World & I*, March 1998, p. 186.

Chapter 2: Leprechaun Sightings

6. Curran, *The Truth About the Leprechaun*, 2000, p. 42.
7. Quoted in Jerome Clark, *Unexplained! 347 Strange Sightings, Incredible Occurrences and Puzzling Physical Phenomena*. Detroit: Visible Ink, 1993.
8. Quoted in Stephen Wagner, "Canoe Trip to the Unknown," *About: Paranormal Phenomena*. http://paranormal.about.com/cs/othercreatures/a/aa070703_p.htm.

9. Quoted in Wagner, "Canoe Trip to the Unknown."
10. Quoted in Wagner, "Canoe Trip to the Unknown."
11. Quoted in Wagner, "Canoe Trip to the Unknown."

Chapter 3: Tricks and Treasure

12. Quoted in Henry Glassie, *Irish Folk Tales*. New York: Pantheon, 1985, p. 165.
13. Quoted in Glassie, *Irish Folk Tales*, p. 165.

Chapter 4: Curse of the Leprechaun

14. Quoted in Jerome Clark, *Extraordinary Encounters: An Encyclopedia of Extraterrestrials and Other-Worldly Beings*. Santa Barbara, CA: ABC-Clio, 2000, p. 103.
15. Quoted in W.B. Yeats, *A Treasury of Irish Myth, Legend and Folklore*. New York: Gramercy, 1986, p. 85.
16. Quoted in Clark, *Unexplained!*, p. 116.

Glossary

bib-and-braces: Protective clothing similar to overalls.

bogs: Areas of wet, spongy land where moss and peat grow.

foulmouthed: Using obscene or filthy language.

Gaelic: A language native to Ireland.

gender: The state of being male or female.

Lucifer: A fallen angel also known as Satan.

mortal: A being subject to death.

nobleman: A man of noble rank.

Otherworld: A world or existence beyond this earthly reality.

poteen: Illegal Irish whiskey.

rushes: Tall, grasslike plants that grow in bogs and swamps.

sod: A section of grassy soil held together by roots.

solitary: Existing or living alone.

For Further Exploration

Books

Yvonne Carroll, *Leprechaun Tales*. Dublin, Ireland: Gill & Macmillan, 2001. This illustrated book includes six magical tales of "little people" and their mischievous interactions with mortals.

Ita Daly, *Irish Myths and Legends*. Oxford, UK: Oxford University Press, 2006. Modern retelling of ten traditional tales of bravery, magic, fairies, and leprechauns.

Miles Harvey, *Look What Came from Ireland*. Danbury, CT: Franklin Watts, 2003. Explores many things that came from Ireland, including holidays, food, sports, musical instruments, and leprechauns.

Kathleen Krull, *A Pot o' Gold: A Treasury of Irish Stories, Poetry, Folklore, and (of Course) Blarney*. New York: Hyperion, 2004. This full-color book contains fun information about Ireland, its land, food, music, limericks, riddles, and myths, including fairies and leprechauns.

Web Sites

Hidden Ireland, a Guide to Irish Fairies (www. irelandseye.com/animation/intro.html). Explores myths about seven Irish fairies, including pookas, changelings, and leprechauns.

Leprechaun Watch (www.irelandseye.com/leprechaun /leprechaun.htm). Internet viewers are invited to keep watch on leprechauns and other fairy activities through a Webcam set up in Ireland.

Lucky Charms Interactive Game (www.luckycharms. millsberry.com). Site features a treasure map with different games and adventures to play.

Index

About the Author

Lori Mortensen is the author of more than 100 stories and articles for children that have appeared in magazines such as *Highlights for Children, Ladybug, Wild Outdoor World*, and many others. She has also written five nonfiction books, including *Basilisks* in KidHaven Press's Monsters series. Mortensen lives in northern California with her husband, three teenagers, three cats, four fish, and her son's slithering ball python.